GLOBAL BEST SOURCING

A tech-company must have for maximising profits and eliminating stress

by Kelvin Davis

GLOBAL BEST SOURCING

A tech-company must have for maximising profits and eliminating stress

by Kelvin Davis

 **Business Freedom Lifestyle**

2014

Copyright © 2014 by Kelvin Davis

All rights reserved. This book or any portion thereof may not be reproduced or used in any manner whatsoever without the express written permission of the publisher except for the use of brief quotations in a book review or scholarly journal.

Fourth Revision. Printed: 2014

ISBN 978-1-291-77469-6

Business Freedom Lifestyle
Focal Point 2nd Floor
18 Second Avenue
COTTON TREE, Queensland, Australia, 4558
www.businessfreedomlifestyle.com

Ordering Information:
Special discounts are available on quantity purchases by corporations, associations, educators, and others. For details, contact the publisher at the above listed address.

U.S. trade bookstores and wholesalers: Please contact Business Freedom Lifestyle Tel: +61(0) 7 3503 6835 Fax: +61(0) 7 5492 8822 or email sales@businessfreedomlifestlye.com

The trademarks used in this book are owned by BFL Limited licensed for use by Business Freedom Lifestyle.
Greymouse trademark printed with permission.
Merendi, and Sunshine Coast Pet Resort logos are printed with permission. Skype®, Microsoft® and
Lync® trademarks are owned by their respective brands.

Dedication

To my mother Lily Davis, thank you for your patience during my school days.

To the best wife in the world, Marisa Wiman thank you for your support.

Without both of you special ladies, I would have never achieved my dream

Contents

Acknowledgements ix

Preface xi

Introduction 1

Chapter 1: Partner Selection 3

Chapter 2: Confidentiality 13

Chapter 3: Reliability 19

Chapter 4: Time or Fixed Price? 25

Chapter 5: Communications 33

Chapter 6: Opening Hours 39

Chapter 7: No Competition 43

Chapter 8: Discovered? 47

Chapter 9: Qualification Alone? 51

Chapter 10: How do I Profit? 55

Appendix 1 – Questions & Answers 61

Appendix 2 - About the Author 67

Appendix 3 – Tour, Sharing Ideas 69

Appendix 4 - Learn More 71

Appendix 5 – Supporter 81

Glossary 84

Acknowledgements

I would like to thank my old bosses, from Mr Ron Schmidt my first boss, and the last Mrs Margareta Coleman. I have learnt so much about business and customer service from you.

During recent times I have met and learnt from international business experts that have made a massive difference in my life.

Robert Kiyosaki	Donald Trump
Kim Kiyosaki	Kerwin Rae
Ken McElroy	Tom Wheelwright

The above group taught me how to find and implement their secrets. I have learnt that success is 'freedom from the restraints of time and money'. Now I find pleasure in helping other technology business owners achieve freedom and cash flow in their business

Preface

This book is written for the following types of company owners using industry specific terminology.

- Information technology
- Cloud installation and supply
- Software development
- Businesses that are heavily dependent on technology

Technology Businesses

Are you getting the best out of your business life? It is your life, so it is always your choice. In everything you do you 'will choose'.

If you own your business you choose your business, industry, customers, vendors, partners and personal lifestyle. Yes it is your choice. In this book I will plant seeds, germinate ideas that can help you expand and grow your Tech Business. When planned correctly this will free up you working time and then your lifestyle.

If your business is technology based, there are so many ways you can improve your business and lifestyle.My name is Kelvin Davis and having worked in the technology industry for over 20 years, I have watched the industry change and evolve in the most amazing way.

I have enjoyed owning my own businesses for over 14 years. During this time I have learnt many hard and valuable lessons, then passed the experience on by helping many entrepreneurs establish and run their own businesses. We all hit the hard road while learning lessons, and now I consider it a privilege to share my experiences, and the ones of other Tech businesses with you.

Now I stand for Freedom and Cash flow in your business which will ultimately present you with an opportunity to live your life to the fullest. It requires training, focus and support; but with the correct mindset, it is possible to achieve anything you want in life.

Like everyone else, I have made and will continue to make mistakes. But I look at these mistakes as learning opportunities and the lessons learnt have certainly made a valuable difference. We learn the most through doing and sharing business insights with others.

The tough questions

The difficult questions you need to ask yourself to find honest answers,

- Do you want to work each and every day in Technology?

- Are your profits lower than what you like?
- Are you fulfilling your true destiny?

It makes no difference whether you write code, support applications, create a website, fix computers, build networks or develop sales and support systems, whatever technology discipline you are doing, are you truly satisfied in your daily work and business? Do you feel your true potential is being utilised to its fullest?

As a business owner you work 8 – 12 hours per day but is this your total life's enjoyment? If you want to live a millionaire's lifestyle now (or in 90 days) and be free from the chains of traditional time for money constraints, I can and will share answers with you. Right here! Right now!

The truth

Often, you have the capability to compete against the larger Software companies or Tech businesses, however lack the resources. This is a mind limitation that larger business try to make you believe.

The truth is you have the power right now, right at your fingertips. Change your thoughts and you can change your life.

Virtual Success Recipe

I focus on how to help business owners grow in this flattening world, by integrating virtual teams into business. The virtual workforce uses one of the key wealth creation principles called *Other Peoples Time* (OPT). THIS is a multiplier for you and your business that gives you massive leverage, if handled correctly.

This book will prove to be a valuable source of ideas, with relevant questions and answers if you are a service based business.

In service industries we offer value to our clients every day, every hour and every minute. You are paid based on the amount of value you provide. Give massive value and you will be rewarded.

I openly share lessons, successes and failures to help your business succeed. Enjoy.

www.kelvindavis.com.au

www.businessfreedomlifestyle.com

www.greymouse.com.au

 **Hot Tips** are placed within this book to describe critical points or money and time saving ideas.

Kelvin Davis

Introduction

Virtual Keys

If you own a technology based business, you would have watched your hardware sales dry up over the last year and software sales being threatened by cloud competitors. Consumer and business software demand shifts almost daily and your service revenue plummets due to fierce competition.

You are working long hours, no time and often no life. Even though you know that the market has changed, you may find yourself struggling to compete.

It makes little difference if you are in the business of software development, website development, infrastructure, programmer, security or operating systems. This market has changed so fast over the last year it can make your head spin! I often meet tech companies confused and worried about the future of their businesses, then I start sharing what other businesses are doing.

When the business employs contractors or full time staff, your challenges grow. Euphoria sets in, and then quickly the expenses start to rise. Often, owners give up in frustration saying that it just does not work.

In this book I will take you through common Virtual Outsourcing challenges for technical based SME businesses, then show you how to overcome these challenges making this outsourcing process work for you.

This is a 'one flight book' designed to teach the business owner what you need while waiting at the airport or travelling on the short flight. It is short, sharp and to the point.

Chapter 1: Partner Selection

Wedded Bliss or Disaster?

Picking the right partner can mean success or failure in your relationship, marriage, business, banker, clients, vendors or friends.

Selecting the right partner is a joy, selecting the wrong one means you are heading for a messy divorce.

The outsourcing choices basically comes down to four flavours or options:

1. Contractor, Elance® – Odesk®
2. Part time / full time resource
3. Working with a partner
4. Purchase a Service

The largest assumption people make is that when they take on a virtual person the problems will be solved. This assumption will lead to disappointment, and often failure.

Here is the truth, selecting a virtual person does not take you away

Global Best Sourcing

from your management responsibilities.

Contractor

When you engage a contractor either directly or through O-Desk® or E-lance®, you have to allocate time to manage the project and person. I have done this myself for a specific purpose or outcome. Always remember they report directly to you (as the project owner) day or night. You will need to allocate time each day to manage the contractor and their deliverables.

Remember, the person is working for you and what they deliver on an hourly, daily or weekly bases is your responsibility, not theirs. The remote person will sit and wait for your instructions. They are project based people. So if the arrangement is not working, analyse where it is going wrong and how to improve now or next time.

When you accept the job is completed in O-Desk or E-lance, only then can the person be paid. Remember the contractor is looking for more work so mostly they just disappear onto the next project. There is no recourse on the task. If you try to get any modifications completed, the challenges start. This form of contractor engagement works well with specific project tasks.

Part time / Full time

While a part time resource sounds cheaper, a full time resource is usually dedicated or focused on your business. I have always seen greater quality results with full time staff. Be aware some 'full time' resources actually work two (2) jobs from home to gain more income. Personally, I prefer to have the remote team in an office that I can watch and observe. Observation and verification can be easily done via web based IP camera's or Skype ® communications.

Partner (Supplier)

Partner supplier is like a close friend that you enter into a Joint Venture. This trusted supplier is selected so that you work very closely for a common goal. While still a supplier, you have open and honest conversations about your business challenges and opportunities. A high level of trust is required in these relationships.

Working with a partner that provides the office space, redundant internet links, generators, UPS ensures a greater level of resource availability to a home based worker. Consider that

Global Best Sourcing

third world countries can have up to 14 power outages per month plus 5 or more extended internet outages. This level of infrastructure reliability (or unreliability) is dependent on the country and partner you select.

Service Partner

Purchasing a service with a Service Level Agreement (SLA) is the final option where the provider takes on the responsibility for ensuring the team is available and working. While the cost is more, the SLA partner handles the delivery.

Consider that some countries have many HR challenges including days absent from work. An example of differences between countries:

- 21 public holidays
- 20 days' vacation leave
- 10 days sick leave
- 3 days bereavement leave

In your decision, remember to factor in the recruitment, interviews, training, monitoring, HR management and reporting costs in any outsourcing strategy.

Kelvin Davis

Resource Management

If you engage a virtual human resource directly, you still will need to manage the person, and receive reports on a weekly basis. Monitoring the Key Performance Indicators (KPI's = output or results) is critical.

Remember that power can be lost up to 14 times per month (in some countries) so a generator is necessary. An Uninterrupted power Supply (UPS – battery backup of power) will not last long enough to cover most outages. A generator and UPS is required in these places to ensure reliability. Also internet connections (links) are often unreliable therefore a home based person will work only when they are on line. When they are not on line, they are usually not billing you and great, unless you have urgent deliverable tasks. Check if the basic utilities are suitable to your business need. I have experienced power and internet provider outages of up to 5 consecutive days so it will at some point interrupt your project, unless you are prepared.

Using an 'outsourcing partner', results in removal of the direct personnel interview, equipment, management and facilities that you want controlled, however many items will still be within your direct supervision.

Global Best Sourcing

Partners can offer the option of alleviating the need for you to handle the 'lower level' management tasks including;

- Redundancy to cover public holidays, sick leave, annual leave, bereavement leave
- Payroll, taxes, superannuation, workers compensation
- Overtime, penalty rates, weekend rates, travel allowance, meal allowances
- Daily working hour reports
- HR functions, including interviewing, selection, employment contracts, KPI management personal development reviews, disciplinary letters
- Office environment including desk, computer, software, electricity, Internet links.
- Telephone systems,
- Providing a secure working environment.
- Facilities management
- Generators, UPS
- Up to 24/7 support expansion options
- Staff travelling options (Some countries are unsafe to travel at night)

The 5 keys to selecting a contractor, dedicated person, partner or service, is to decide if you want to:

1. Dedicate the time to micro manage
2. Outsource the management function
3. Partner to manage the human resource demands of a virtual person
4. Manage deliverables or time-based resources
5. Lower cost for the service to be delivered

When you start communicating with your outsourcing partner, check if they provide a full package service, or HR management function. Investigate if there are any extra costs.

Remember HR management will ensure the person is available and on time. The tasks that you want completed and reporting are managed by yourself. (Unless you purchase a service)

Global Best Sourcing

Hardware / Software costs

Extra costs can also be added on for computer equipment from some providers including additional RAM, software, multiple screens or better quality headsets. Check first, as extra costs usually come 3 – 9 weeks after commencement.

Example - Testimonial from Ordyss, Brisbane (an 8-year outsourcing business partner).

Ordyss commenced using (Greymouse) **outsourcing** *resources in 2006, to resolve a short term staff shortage challenge. This has grown over the years into a long term working relationship - adding value to our customer service delivery.*

Keith Lavelle – Managing Director Ordyss.

Kelvin Davis

The Right Partner

Choosing the right outsourcing partner can be compared to finding the right lifetime partner. Just like personal relationships take your time with a long engagement. Rushing the courtship often results in unhappy couples.

The right partner will make your life blissful and be with you forever; however a wrong selection can end in a messy and costly divorce.

> *"Everybody needs a **partner** to stand right by their side. Not only down for the good times. But also right down through to the bad times"* Will Smith

Global Best Sourcing

Chapter 2: Confidentiality

Your business Intellectual Property (I.P.) comprises of at least,

- Customer databases
- The way you do business
- Your procedures
- Your documentation
- Your logo and name

Protection of your business I.P. and end-customers is critical to any successful support.

The confidentiality agreement or promise needs to ensure that your business systems are protected. The best way is to use a 'confidentiality promise' or confidentiality agreement that continues for a minimum of three (3) years beyond the conclusion of the relationship.

Nowadays any data breach is liable on both you and the outsourcing partner. Be very aware that your Professional Indemnity / Professional liability (PI/PL) insurance are liable for any potential loss. If you have a supplier partner company with PI/PL insurance of at least $10,000,000, it reduces your own PI/PL insurance premium costs and minimises your potential liability.

Global Best Sourcing

An added benefit of a "Confidentiality Agreement" is that you mitigate the risk by ensuring that the information provided to the contractor remains confidential.

If your clients are sensitive, take the next step of asking for a Police Clearance on all the staff that work on your clients. This way it ensures another level of protection.

Critical areas:

- Your company procedures and policies remain confidential
- Your administration accounts and password details are safe
- Any potential breach or password risk is mitigated immediately
- Data remains in the country, only support is relocated

The 6 things you need to include in your confidentiality agreement for business protection.

1. Client lists & client personal details
2. Personal information that may include current or historical company or individual records
3. ABN, A.C.N. T.I.N. taxation records or company number(s)
4. Debt collection, credit reference or credit card details
5. Data processing, systems, web site portals, or procedures
6. Company procedures, instructions or company Intellectual Property (IP)

This ensures your virtual partner and its staff maintain the highest values.

The confidentially agreement must also be reflected or passed on from the partner to their employees with a formal employment agreement.

You can always check to see that the partner has employment agreements and that it is legitimate in its responsibilities.

Global Best Sourcing

Risk of Lost Data Reported In BBC News

Welsh councils are not doing enough to protect people's confidential data from falling into the wrong hands, according to the UK information watchdog.

Eight of Wales' 22 councils have had cases of data being lost or stolen in the last three years.

The Information Commissioner's Office (ICO) in Wales says it has "deep concern".

Councils involved have told BBC Wales they have taken data protection seriously and therefore have tightened procedures.
http://www.bbc.co.uk/news/uk-wales-16147470

A confidentiality agreement is like a pre-nuptial (pre-marriage agreement). It is prepared in a state of calm positive attitude between the partners. You hope never to need it, but you sure are glad you had one when it comes to parting ways.

> *"My husband and I didn't sign a pre-nuptial agreement. We signed a mutual suicide pact".* – Rosanne Barr

Global Best Sourcing

Example of a Confidentially Promise.

Chapter 3: Reliability

The partner you select needs to be contactable at all times.

I have personally listened to horror stories where the company was unable to locate or contact the virtual resources. Imagine having a major issue and the person is not contactable or only on delayed email responses. They may have setup passwords, access, or sent broadcast emails, or worse still, have done something bordering on illegal.

Partner Verification

Often over 40% of applicants applying for work with Greymouse or other Service Providers have never been assigned a local government tax number (T.I.N.). As a result, we help the applicant complete the government forms to work legally. That way the employee and company remain legal complying with all the local laws. As you will notice by the high percentage, many businesses and workers do not comply with the local laws.

To verify if the employee is going to remain in your service, and the partner is abiding by the

Global Best Sourcing

countries rules, just ask for the employees T.I.N. number (Tax Identification Number). The reason to ask this question, is that many substandard business or contractors do not pay the countries taxes (PAYG, PAYE, Superannuation / 401K, Phil Health, SSS etc). As a result they can disappear (closing up their office) when an auditor suddenly appears on their doorstep.

Your business does not want to be left without resources and worse still without ample notice so this quick check verifies the partner is legitimate within the country.

Also be careful of companies employing relatives or close friends of a current virtual worker. In many countries family comes first, work and business second. When the time comes for one person to move, the group often decides to relocate all the relatives together. Choose carefully and not just relatives of a current employee.

You must have the confidence that the provider can track the employee down, and in the unusual cases, have the power to take legal action when and where necessary.

Kelvin Davis

This disciplined approach can be done by court stamped documents or having a Human Resource Lawyer on the partner's team.

If employing a person directly, having multiple methods of contact such as email, local phone number, Skype name, backup person, manager and local account manager removes any unwanted surprises.

The partner's resources can easily have an alertness test by doing the following:

- Appointments are on time
- High degree of accuracy on all tasks
- Answering calls consistently within 2 or 3 rings
- Completing tasks on time
- Raising potential issues early
- Following an escalation process

Global Best Sourcing

The 5 mistakes to avoid when evaluating virtual resources:

1. Often people only do what is 'inspected' and not what is 'expected'. (Include a daily, weekly or monthly report.)
2. Not having a reporting loop to check status of work or projects.
3. Assumptions
    a. Assuming the rules applied are the same as your own country
    b. Assuming a 'yes' means 'Yes'.
4. If you are trying to find out if they have understood your instructions, just ask for instructions to be repeated back to you in their own words and terms.

Example - I particularly liked the flexibility to assist when we are short on staff, and I have been very impressed by the professionalism of the management and their staff. During the last few months, we expanded the service to include essential problem resolution when necessary. – Tech Business (name withheld)

Kelvin Davis

Having a partner and virtual resources that you can trust, rely on and depend upon, helps you achieve immense freedom in your business. If you are a single person business; it allows you to leave, focus on sales and grow the business at a rapid pace. This beautiful transformation is just like the caterpillar evolving into a cocoon and then emerging as a butterfly. While it takes a little time, the business transformation is permanent and astounding.

> *"A true friend never breaches the trust of his companion or stabs him in his back. He is trustworthy and reliable."* – Sam Veda

Global Best Sourcing

Chapter 4: Time or Fixed Price?

Savings is certainly an important factor but should never be the first consideration in the partner or resource selection. Often businesses ask for 'time based billing' instead of fixed cost. In the long run it never works out effectively and the person completing the work is then looking for new work and money.

In my experience fixed price for the support is less complex and results in a more effective use of the virtual resource than time and materials. Consider that they are also looking for a reliable steady job to feed their families.

Remember, the saving you received from offshore is large by comparison to a local person.

Generally, the saving is approximately 40% of employing a local person to complete the same task. Savings are higher if you include the superannuation, workers compensation, electricity, software, computers, office facilities and other supporting costs.

To compare local verses remote resources, check the savings include:

Global Best Sourcing

- Superannuation
- Workers compensation
- Electricity
- Desk
- Office Rent
- Computer
- 2 screens
- PC & PC Software licenses

When comparing partners or selecting your supplier also checks these items:

- Staff retention policies
- Events, monthly or yearly
- Medical insurance
- Employment agreement clawback (in case of exam payments)
- Holiday leaves
- Compliance with local laws (do employees have a T.I.N. – Tax Identification Number)
- Number of vacation days, public holidays, sick leave, bereavement leave
- Penalty rates if working a public holiday
- Air conditioned offices
- Desk size
- Water supplied

- Christmas party costs
- Computer – operating system, RAM, Headset
- 2 x screens (For efficiency)
- PC Software licenses
- Bond payment, upfront payments
- Currencies and exchange rate costs

The 4 elements of fixed cost resources over time and materials:

1. Tracking times, verifying times
2. Known budgetary amount
3. Reduced administration costs
4. Customer satisfaction as the key driver (not number of hours worked)
5. Removes money focus (Working extra hours for more $)

Global Best Sourcing

Here are 4 reasons why 'time for money' or costs by the hour is a simple way of doing business however will hurt you long term. Transition your mentality to a fixed price mindset, as it encourages your business growth.

1. **It shackles your profits.**
   If your business income or revenue is in any way linked to your time, your business model is fundamentally flawed; The reasons being:
   a. There are only so many hours in the day and eventually, you will price yourself out of your markets reach.
   b. You drastically reduce your value, throttling your earning potential.

   Your provider will strike the same barriers.

2. **It creates a conflict of interest.** The more efficient you are, the greater your time savings. Less efficient, costs more. As a consumer, if I am paying a service provider by the hour, the longer it takes them to deliver the result, the better off they are. **Good for them, but bad for me**. Time based billing literally

puts buyers and sellers at odds with each other.

3. **Retards creativity and innovation.**
   Now to look at your business, the faster you work as a service provider to deliver a result, the worse off you are.

   If the market won't allow you to charge more per hour, where is the incentive to do better? There is none. In my mind this is crazy!

4. **It's anti-entrepreneurial.**
   Entrepreneurs strive to work "**on their business'**, not "**in their business**". If you charge by the hour you're literally building yourself into your business - handcuffing yourself to deliver value every day. YOU HAVE A JOB, not a business.

Worse still, when you stop working (through sickness or holidays), your business stops earning which strips the value from the very company you're trying to build.

Global Best Sourcing

The alternative to the evils of billing for your time is to convert your skills and services into value based products and outsource up to 95% of the tasks. The market will value a packaged result far more than it will your time.

Example (Name withheld) - Early this year, we expanded our services to include server event error checks & diagnosis, test restores and antivirus verifications all completed on a daily basis. This takes our proactive support to a new level of service not possible with standard monitoring software. The additional service taken-on, was hassle free and completed within a week. Savings come from a more reliable infrastructure platform, less customer downtime plus 30% labor cost savings

The difference is the same as chalk and cheese. Once you have experienced the flavour of a full service at a fixed price, you will never attempt to consume cheaply again.

> *"A penny saved is a penny earned."* Benjamin Franklin

Kelvin Davis

Global Best Sourcing

Chapter 5: Communications

Instant communication with the partner resources or management is a key component to your business success!

Customer service is vital and built on quick efficient communications. When used effectively, end business support becomes seamless and integrated. Any potential issues are resolved quickly and efficiently. It is inevitable that issues will arise and when they do, this instant communication will quickly ensure it is resolved.

Some of the most efficient communication methods:

- Skype - voice and video
- Voip - number provided by the partner
- Lync - instant messaging, voice and video
- Conference calling – for multi-party
- The engineers email and / or the partners email system (as a backup)
- Mobile phone numbers

- Participation of remote engineers in team meeting; using conference calls.

Global Best Sourcing

- Managers escalation details
- Onsite and off-site group meetings (conference calls)

The 3 keys to successful communication integration:

- Instant responses (IM, Phone or email within 20 minutes)
- Personalised service (empathy, correctly formatted and not a machine)
- Follow-up (Ongoing communication)

You remain responsible for communication with your team members. Constant and regular communication works.

Kelvin Davis

Example – Markinson

As we rapidly approach the end of 2010, I would like to thank you for your ongoing partnership and support throughout the year. Together, we've delivered and supported innovative solutions and services to hundreds of Markinson customers.

This support has helped us to grow significantly in 2010 and has contributed to Markinson proudly winning several coveted awards. We expect to see this growth and level of customer commitment continue in 2011 with many new projects already in planning.
Ian Whiting C.E.O.

Just as communication between partners forms the basis of a solid marriage, open communication in a business relationship ensures success. Conversely, failure to communicate effectively leads to a messy divorce and failure in business.

Global Best Sourcing

> "The most common mistake couples make while trying to resolve conflicts, is to respond before they have the full picture. This inevitably leads to arguments. When people respond too quickly, they often respond to the wrong issue. Listening helps us focus on the heart of the conflict. When we listen, understand, and respect each other's ideas, we can then find a solution in which both of us are winners."
>
> (Dr Gary Chapman, from the article, "Solving Conflicts Without Arguing, featured in the Summer 2007 issue of Marriage Partnership Magazine)
> http://www.marriagemissions.com/quotes-on-communication-and-conflict/

Kelvin Davis

Global Best Sourcing

Chapter 6: Opening Hours

Your customers will buy at a time and place of their choosing, not yours. Since the internet competition is so fierce, why not have the capability to respond and answer the instant your customers want you? This way you gain more trust and a competitive advantage over the competition.

Check your partner has expansion options for up to and including 24 hours per day, 7 days a week. This gives your business a competitive edge by increasing customer contact, customers and then revenue when you need it.

Selecting a partner that cannot give you these options restricts your potential for expansion. Therefore, it is vital to consider this early. Typically, a high level of engineering skill is not required after hours; however, monitoring and resolution of basic issues puts you leaps and bounds ahead of the competition.

A good partner will offer a 'Network Operations Centre' service (NOC) as part of their options.

Global Best Sourcing

Expanded service will provide:

- 24 hours monitoring
- Internet attack response
- Escalation path
- Backup issue resolution
- Contact point

The four rules for after hour expansion:

- Market demands 24/7, be prepared now
- Lower skills at night, high level available on call by the provider
- Visual monitoring and response
- Following an escalation process

Example – *Monitoring Service 24/7 (name withheld)*

"The savings are extraordinary, to even consider offering 24hrs solution locally. It would easily cost in the vicinity of $200,000 U.S. The Greymouse solution is considerably less and easy to manage."

"The biggest challenge is getting our systems and processes right. We have been tuning this

Kelvin Davis

over the last few months, improving service delivery."

"Greymouse provides us with skilled resources to leverage, while I concentrated on our sales growth. The Greymouse team allowed us to provide a service offering without breaking the bank."

Greymouse

Having a team of the little elves or Santa's helpers that work through the night, silently and effectively, leads to excellent results the next day and gives you peace of mind.

Global Best Sourcing

> *"The best advisers, helpers and friends, always are not those who tell us how to act in special cases, but who give us, out of themselves, the ardent spirit and desire to act right, and leave us then, even through many blunders, to find out what our own form of right action is."* Philip Brooks
>
> http://thinkexist.com/quotation/the_best_advisers-helpers_and_friends-always_are/166689.html

Chapter 7: No Competition

Partners that compete with your customers threaten your survival.

Software suppliers are notorious for by-passing the business or channel then engaging or selling directly to your customers. Ensuring that the partner you select does not have a local support team results in the fact they will not be able to provide the same level of support that you do.

A virtual engineering partner should and must stay that way, virtual! Your partner should only be supplying the technical skills to you, and then it is only you that does the reselling to your client base.

Minimise the competitive threat by;

- A strong confidentially agreement, identifying non-competing sections
- Work with a partner, not an individual person
- Obtain partner references
- Your company IP (systems & process) is updated monthly and returned to you as part of the monthly report

Global Best Sourcing

Include the following 3 key sections in the confidentiality agreement, to ensure the virtual partner is not a competitive threat:

Example – Confidentially promise

1. We promise to treat as confidential and keep secret all statements (oral or written), client information, records, statements, procedures, contracts, agreements, specifications, reports, documents, knowledge and information.

2. We promise to return all documents and other materials embodying, or in any way relating to, the Information, including any authorised copies or reproductions of such documents and other materials made by either party, and shall destroy or render unusable all details of, or in any way relating to, The Information held in databases or in other electronic storage or retrieval systems, either:
   a. on demand, or
   b. without demand as soon as the same is no longer required

Kelvin Davis

3. The terms of this Promise shall apply for a period of 3 years from the date of this document or earlier if both parties agree to terminate it in writing.

Interview with Caretech

Are you concerned with data sovereignty and intellectual property protection?

"Not really concerned. All our data is stored in Australia, located in secure data centers. All access is via Remote access technology. As for intellectual property, it wasn't really a concern for us we keep the data local and support goes remote. We retain control"

Knowing your supplier cannot directly compete for your customers, gives you peace of mind and a sense of control over your business direction. Nothing hurts your business more than an employee or business partner stabbing you in the back, taking your most valued customers.

Global Best Sourcing

> *"That's why God put non-compete clauses in contracts"* Mad Men 2007 Lyons gate.
> Video available here:
> http://www.hark.com/mad-men/thats-why-god-put-non-compete-clauses-in-contracts

Chapter 8: Discovered?

The customer has discovered that you use a virtual workforce in your business, so what!

We have discovered that it is more important to have the customer problem resolved now, than to wait for 12 hours until someone returns to the office. In our measurements, 98% of people do not care about the location of the support, as long as their issue is resolved immediately and the person handling their issue has a pleasant accent and is responsive.

In our experience we have found:

- The voice system is critical to ensure seamless conversations (no time delays during conversations)
- The customer prefers to be told the truth
- Fiji is a favourite destination for holidays and accepted by end clients
- South Pacific accent is acceptable to Australian and New Zealand populations
- After six months of great support from the team members, they just do not care

Global Best Sourcing

- Less than 1.2% of the business population is concerned about location
- Philippines is now becoming more acceptable, (with their American accent)

The 3 critical factors for customer acceptance:

- Voice quality must be at a very good standard. After testing multiple systems we have created our own Asterisk (Voice) PBX system and backup facility to ensure the best possible quality and resiliency. Voice systems must also comply with international telecommunication laws.
- If the end customer asks about the support location, tell the truth.
- Responsiveness to end customer concerns

Testimonial when Cardno moved from a virtual (Fiji) support to an internal support model.

I already miss you guys, more than you know. I hope the Cardno IT Group is as efficient as you all have been. I will miss Ronald most of

Kelvin Davis

all, give him a goodbye kiss for me. One day, I hope to meet him in person, so this isn't goodbye.

Yes, I do want to stay friends. I will contact you after the migration; it will give us another topic of conversation over lunch.

Thanks again to you both, Clinton, Ronald & Jiji and all your staff, your friendly customer service puts you ahead of the rest..

Till then, take care.
Regards,
Patricia McDonald
Laboratory administrator / IT manager
CARDNO BOWLER

No one likes being lied to; especially a partner or a customer. If lied to, it leaves a sense of distrust. If your clients do not ask, nothing is said as it is not important to them. If they ask, we always provide the truth of our team member's location. When set up correctly, less than 1.8 % ever work out that the support is remote.

"Honesty is the best policy" – Anonymous

Global Best Sourcing

Chapter 9: Qualification Alone?

Qualifications alone will not work!

The company you work with will ensure that you are provided the correct resource to perform the tasks you need. Employing a high level engineering / designer / programmer to a helpdesk role will create a massive mismatch that is neither efficient, sustainable nor productive.

Using a helpdesk resource for the basics and a higher skilled engineer on tasks in which he is an expert in, yields the best results. Each has been trained to perform their role the best.

Your partner will:

- Select the best resource and give them basic and quality training
- Ensure they have industry certifications (that may be passed onto your business)
- Provide technology update training
- Teach your methodology to one person, and the partner ensures internal training to give redundancy
- Do a cultural match, as sometimes cultures are shy or sensitive

Global Best Sourcing

The 3 success rules:

- It takes time to understand your clients, usually between 3 – 4 months before you can completely be at ease with them.
- Sometimes phrases need to be translated for effectiveness. (Examples, 'a once over,' 'a vanilla install' mean nothing to other countries.)
- Knowledge plus experience gives wisdom.

First of all, I would like to thank you and Marisa for the overwhelming support you have provided Fiji Fish for the last few months. If you would not have come in, I do not know what would have happened.

Secondly, your staff were excellent in their work. I was given every tiny bit of information at every stage of my project and they made me understand what was actually happening. I always received positive responses from them whereby I got bit worried when the migration of servers came in.

Kelvin Davis

Their feedback was very prompt as per my request. I did not find any difficulty in communicating with the team, in fact, any other staff from your office that did assist me during the projects.

I look forward in working with you and hope that Fijifish will have a pleasant relationship ahead. ***Jiten***

If a person is 'green behind the ears' they can prove to be damaging to your relationship with your business clients. It is better to have a partner with enough experience to identify such inexperienced people and help them learn and mature before they allow them to deal with your clients.

> Trust the partner's wisdom of how to make outsourcing work.

Global Best Sourcing

> *"Knowledge + Experience = Wisdom"* –
> *Kelvin Davis*

Chapter 10: How do I Profit?

Understanding the numbers is fundamental to any business. In this example we have a software business that currently has customer support 24 hours per day, 7 days a week, 365 days per year for their corporate business application.

For the Active time zones the customers included New Zealand and Australia, logged into the support system and if a high priority exists, escalated. Customers wanted to communicate using phone, email and SMS.

The company required 4 full time staff to deliver this service, however they are not fully utilized after business hours.

Comparing the cost of service delivery we see the savings,

24/7 Resources	Australian	Outsourced
4 x FTE	$200,000	$49,000

Table notes
- FTE (Full Time Employee)
- On costs included and rounded

The company turnover was $1,500,000 resulting in an immediate saving of $151,000 or

Global Best Sourcing

9.9% profit net profit increase. The customer relocated one of the support team in to sales increasing revenue.

Implementation of the outsourcing support model took 30 days and the savings commenced within the second month.

With the savings the business expanded marketing activities to include Canada and the USA resulting in increasing sales and minimal support costs.

How was this possible?

The customer used support structure with a guaranteed Service Level Agreement. The client did not want the H.R. recruitment, training, vacation, sick leave (headaches) or resourcing issues that comes with direct overseas employment.

Supporting end client technology or applications becomes simple when systems and documentations are created and then implemented by the provider.

The key is to document the processes (Systems), escalation and procedures that you need followed. When completed, this becomes a part of your business Intellectual Property, thereby increasing the value of your business. The escalation process to Internet Providers, Engineers, suppliers and vendors becomes critical for a quick and accurate support.

Key information needed for supporting remotely:

- Your business value (Mission and Vision statements)
- Customer specific requirements
- Induction into your business

The 6 rules for any remote support:

- Pictures of the site, peoples (and equipment if necessary)
- Escalation contact details (Eg internet links, engineer details)
- Network diagrams / software problem-solving slow chart
- Company contact details
- Escalation for support structure
- On site escalation contact details

Also consider the value of the software business (in this example) increases by an investment multiplier. The investor wants a return

Global Best Sourcing

<u>without having to work in</u> the business. The investor wants to see systems and contracts in place that support the complete business.

Case study of Highland Pacific remote monitoring published in the Fiji sun http://www.kelvindavis.com.au/files/Fiji-Sun-17-September-2012.pdf

Now, with Sonar, all of Highlands Pacific's systems and backups are monitored proactively in various ways. CFO, Craig now has greater confidence with his email. Not only that, the staff are able to enjoy a much more stable working environment.

This Sonar technology receives notifications on the status of the systems every minute. If the notification is not received within three minutes, a heartbeat alert is generated and the Sonar team investigates the issue and a notification is sent to Highlands Pacific's IT Partner.

The services Sonar provides have proven to be very beneficial for businesses that depend on technology. Business owners will be at ease knowing that their systems are regularly checked and monitored.

Kelvin Davis

A picture is worth a thousand words! By having pictures of your customers, your team members and location helps break down barriers, allowing the best support possible. Remember it takes teamwork to successfully support your clients.

> *"It is far easier to remember something by association than it is by just cramming it into your head". – Linguistic programming*

Global Best Sourcing

Appendix 1 – Questions & Answers

Common questions and answers provided daily.

Can you take Helpdesk calls?

Yes, the support team takes calls, emails, live chats logging all issues in your helpdesk package. This package is similar to your CRM.

Can you take application support calls?

Yes, an application support call is still a help desk priority. Often we find that a Virtual Assistant performs a better task than a technical person. Then the call is escalated to a technical resource as needed.

Do I need high skill sets?

The highest skill sets should remain in your country and be customer facing. For them to be efficient, the simple tasks need to be assigned to your virtual team members.

Do the support team have an accent?

Yes, most virtual workforces have some form of accent. In 2004 this was a factor influencing customer purchasing decisions, but not anymore.

How do I specify greetings & scripts?

Provide your partner with the greeting scripts of your choice as well as instructions for answering incoming customer calls. That way you will ensure that your calls are answered as your business and your company name. Most important is to maintain your business culture.

How do I divert my phone?

The partner that you use will provide you with a dedicated local phone number. Simply forward your existing phone number (local or Toll Free 1300) to the number allocated to you. If you have a 'local' number all diverted phone calls are low cost.

Can I divert my mobile?

Yes you can. In an iPhone ® it is in 'Settings>Phone>Call Forwarding'. Switch it on, then enter your receptionist number.

Start Taking Calls 24 /7?

Expanding your availability for your clients up to 24 hours per day gives you a competitive advantage in the market. Some virtual providers do not offer this extended hours service, therefore verify they do have this service before you start.

Can you start straight away?

Providers will have some team members under training or on standby ready to start taking your calls. The other option is for you to select your own resources. Basic training of a virtual person takes about 4 – 8 weeks. Test them and ensure they match your need.

The call answering is simple

1. Your customer calls
2. The call is directed to the Voip number
3. Calls are answered by friendly receptionists.
4. If you are available, virtual receptionists instantly transfer important calls directly to your phone (landline or mobile).

Is it easy to physically meet the virtual team?

Yes Fiji at 3.5 hours flying, is easier to reach than the Philippines with 10 – 12 hours travel time. Merendi a Virtual Receptionist client recently visited the Fiji office, sharing her experiences. The family then had a holiday during the trip.

I recently had the pleasure of visiting Fiji to meet Shobna and her team of VRs & VAs and to train my new VA Binita. They were most welcoming when we arrived and made my partner and I feel very much at home. Prior to arriving in Suva Shobna was very helpful in providing information on accommodation where we could stay

Kelvin Davis

and she also organized a taxi to pick us up from the airport to our resort. The team at Greymouse were friendly and were very open to having us visit and work with them for the day. Shobna and her team are always helpful and there is nothing they won't do for you. Their goal is to ensure their clients' needs are met and of course they always exceed this.

Is the business trip tax deductible?

If you already have a business relationship with your virtual team members, and your travel is for the purpose of meeting the team and spending time with them teaching, training or learning what is possible in the virtual world, by definition it is a business related activity.

Check with your accountant on the percentage of the travel expenses and accommodation that becomes business tax deductible, but based on normal practice, it is a percentage of your actual travel costs that you are travelling to, from or remaining in the office area.

The virtual office organized tours that we run are considered 100% tax deductible.

Visit this web site to see the upcoming tour times and dates.
http://www.businessfreedomlifestyle.com

Appendix 2 -About the Author

About Kelvin Davis

Kelvin has a broad depth of international and domestic business Information Technology industry experience including, creation of international companies, establishment of procurement and distribution channels, taxation, export and importation requirements.

His personal business experience comes from owning and managing nine (9) businesses including over sixty (60) staff in four (4) countries. Kelvin founded and manages businesses in Australia, Fiji, New Zealand, Philippines and the South Pacific regions.

Kelvin became an award winning Business Mentor and Milestone Manager for the Queensland Government sponsored Vortex (creative industries), Financing Innovation Growth (FIG) and Bluestorm business training programs coordinated by the Achaeus Group.

Today, Kelvin continues to participate in the Queensland Department of State Development and Innovation Mentoring for Growth (M4G) and Mentoring for Investment (M4I) programs based in Brisbane and Sunshine Coast regions.

As this is Kelvin's first book, he is looking for your feedback. Visit his web site and share your thoughts. www.kelvindavis.com.au

Visit www.greymouse.com.au or call the virtual team members on 1300 20 60 20 (Australia free call) or +61 (0)7 3118 9594 to expand your horizons.

Appendix 3 –Tour, Sharing Ideas

Many businesses ask to see how this virtual workforce works first hand. If you wish to understand behind the scenes action simply arrange a visit. To help business owners, regular tours are conducted through both the Greymouse Fiji and Philippines offices. The tours purpose is to help business owners understand what is possible and explore new opportunities through personal experience and 'Mastermind Days'.

The simplest way to experience what is possible in your business, is to join our organized tour where you meet the support teams face to face. During the tour, business owners learn how freedom and lifestyle choices can be integrated into their businesses creating massive value for clients and the owner.

To learn about freedom and lifestyle choices in your business, visit our membership site on www.businessfreedomlifestyle.com. Tour details dates and bookings are available online.

Appendix 4 - Learn More

Business Freedom Lifestyle Ltd has been established for the purpose of sharing business knowledge to the world. Kelvin Davis and Marisa Wiman founded the company to share the lessons that they, and their clients have learned on their business journeys. The journey is more important than the destination, so these lessons come from business owners that transformed their lives.

Additional books written by Kelvin Davis, Marisa Wiman and published by Business Freedom Lifestyle are identified displayed in this section.

These books are designed to help you on your journey sharing ideas, answering the most commonly asked questions. You can purchase copies of the books from these web sites.

www.businessfreedomlifestyle.com
www.lulu.com

E-book versions are also available from the web sites below. www.kindle.com or www.businessfreedomlifestyle.com

To assist you on your personal wealth creation journey I have a complete list of recommended reading located on this link http://www.businessfreedomlifestyle.com/recommended-reading

Kelvin and Marisa also started Greymouse for the purpose of helping business achieve this goal. As professional outsources and business investors they are constantly looking for new business opportunities.

Kelvin Davis

Speaking events, training and business assistance is available here. www.businessfreedomlifestyle.com

---

To order these products simply,

Phone: +61(0) 7 3503 6835
Fax: +61(0) 7 5492 8822 or
Web: www.businessfreedomlifestyle.com
Email: sales@businessfreedomlifestlyle.com

Business
Freedom
Lifestyle

Action Items and Notes:

Kelvin Davis

10 Key Business Outsourcing Ingredients

Business owners are now faced with challenges where the cost of local labor, and compliance costs outweigh the returns.

Often the business owner gets no return for the hours of hard work, sweat and stress. There is a different way, and Marisa Wiman shares her wealth of outsourcing experience for all.

This is an educational business book from the 'SME Virtual Workforce Queen'. She shares 10 practical guidelines so help you succeed. Included within these pages are;

- What to outsource?
- How do I train the virtual team
- How do I build trust
- Is a countries culture important?
- Language barriers!
- Virtual vs. physical resources
- Full or Part Time
- How to I measure results

- Document systems
- How to manage remotely

This is a one flight book written so you can absorb the critical information within one short plane flight. After all in business time is critical.
ISBN 978-1-291-76878-7

http://www.lulu.com/shop/marisa-wiman/10-key-business-outsourcing-ingredients/paperback/product-21593152.html

Kelvin Davis
The Secret Road to Wealth
Time to Live your Dreams
by Kelvin Davis

Why do some people effortlessly achieve wealth, while others struggle with no cash left at the end of the week?

The secret road to wealth gives you the roadmap the rich use to create freedom and cash flowing into their pockets every single day. This book will teach you how to;

- Crystalize your dreams
- Discover your inspiration, then leverage it
- Set you income, without working for it
- Recognize the pension trap
- Explode the myth 'time for money'
- Understand what creates your reality
- Master the inner game of wealth
- Reveal the money making machines

Kelvin created a freedom business, one that produces money without the owner's time. Then he replicated this same model in his clients businesses, creating freedom and cash flow for the owners. You walk beside Kelvin and his clients as they share lessons learnt on every step of their journeys.

Instead of relying on government false promises, create the life you always dreamed of.

Available from;

>www.lulu.com
>www.businessfreedomlifestyle.com

Kelvin Davis
Secret Keys to Business Success
Create the Life You Want
by Kelvin Davis

The Secret Keys to Business Wealth exposes the reason why some businesses uncap untold wealth while others struggle each day. Understanding the differences between success and failure, then seeing the barriers, gives you unimaginable power.

Kelvin created a freedom business, one that produces money without consuming the owner's time. He then created the same model with his clients. Almost overnight, his owners could travel to exotic countries, or take that well-earned rest.

The secret keys are given to you, explained in simple terms, together with stories of the successful implementation in other industries. Often these small business, range from a single person, (or sometimes without any staff) through to medium size businesses. Imagine learning about this turnkey operation business that just produces income, gives the owner the option of early retirement or allows to expand into other businesses while the team delivers the services needed. Learn how you can implement this in your industry to create new wealth and freedom opportunities.

This book continues from the Secret Road to Wealth teaching about time freedom and cash-flow creating money from business.

>   www.lulu.com
>   www.businessfreedomlifestyle.com

Direct link: http://www.lulu.com/shop/kelvin-davis/secret-keys-to-business-wealth/paperback/product-21624113.html

Appendix 5 – Supporter

The business world is being flattened by economics, technology, demographics and regulations. To win in this flattening world, companies must transform their way of thinking, working, and engagement with partners that help them achieve their goals.

Greymouse Virtual Workforce is an Australian controlled HR provider supplying high quality, time sensitive and cost effective services through its own off-shoring facilities based in Fiji South Pacific and Legazpi, in the Philippines. We maximize the strengths of both countries, plus reduce outsourcing risks, giving our clients a massive head start. This way our customers realize a freedom in their business that can only be dreamt of.

How does it work?

We start slowly to be sure that the systems all work for your business. With a feedback loop we constantly improve and refine systems. Providing customers with a 24 hours and 7 days a week option, we fulfil our objective to give you, the business owner Time Freedom to finish more pressing matters or just relax. We believe in your Business Freedom.

Greymouse Fiji Team Members

Greymouse business transformation team includes
- Virtual Receptionists
- Virtual Assistants
- Techies (Marketing, web site and online specialists)
- Information Technology specialists
- Accountancy / Bookkeeping
- Data Entry team

Kelvin Davis
Greymouse Philippines Team Members

Special trial offer by quoting this book's title

USA Freecall: 1888-7790643
UK Phone: 3308280731
Australia toll free: 1300 206020
International: +61(0) 7 3118 9594
International Fax: +61(0) 7 5492 8822
Web: www.greymouse.com.au
Email: sales@greymouse.com.au

Glossary

A.B.N.   Australian Business Number

A.C.N.   Australian Company Number

Asterisk   Linux Open source voice server.

I.P.   Intellectual Property contains your business knowledge. Essentially it is the way you run your business, logo's, trademarks, systems and procedures for section of your intellectual knowledge.

Lync ®   Microsoft Voice, Instant Messaging and Conference server.

T.I.N.   Tax Identification Number, in Australia it is called a Tax File Number.

VoIP   Voice Over Internet Protocol. Telephone internet connection.

Action Items and Notes:

Action Items and Notes:

Kelvin Davis

www.ingramcontent.com/pod-product-compliance
Lightning Source LLC
Chambersburg PA
CBHW072223170526
45158CB00002BA/729